Watch Out: Bail___ _____

How to deal with the bailiff in today's credit crisis

by D. Silvester G

Second Edition (English Language Version)

Published in the United Kingdom
By Perfect Publishers Ltd 2009

Printed in England by Lightning Source UK Ltd

Cover Design by Duncan Bamford
http://www.insightillustration.co.uk

Edited by Jan Andersen
http://www.creativecopywriter.org

ISBN 978-1-905399-38-3

Perfect Publishers Ltd
23 Maitland Avenue
Cambridge
CB4 1TA
England

www.perfectpublishers.co.uk

Dedication

Dedicated to those who have been made bankrupt, lost their homes, are in debt, or have suffered at the hands of a bailiff through no fault of their own.

Table of Contents

Important Note

Changes of law can happen at any time. Therefore, all the information in this book is to be used as a guide only and it is always recommended that you seek legal advice in the first instance.

Chapter 1

Introduction

British bailiff law is "probably the worst in the world," according to an independent body, which advises ministers on debt collection.

Chairman of the Law Enforcement Reform Group, Philip Evans, was speaking as part of a File on 4 investigation into private firms who collect public debt.

The use of bailiffs has increased significantly over the last decade or so and dates back to the day of the Saxon landlords who used bailiffs against tenants who owed them monies or rent. Distress was used by an officer of the king as a means to enforce an order of the court. From the 16th century onwards, the powers of the bailiff were defined and the limits of distress established.

A bailiff's certificate lasts for 2 years. If or when the bailiff changes employers, or their personal details change during the 2 year period, they must surrender their certificate and a new one will be issued to them with the necessary changes made.

The different types of bailiff and forms of distress used for the collection of the various types of debt and the legal framework in which the bailiffs operate is complex and ill defined, so much so that your local Bobby usually doesn't have a clue of the bailiffs' legal powers. In addition, County Court Bailiffs are in charge of executing warrants of eviction in mortgage and rent cases and the standard rules (e.g. peaceful entry does not apply in these cases).

The purpose of the majority of bailiff action is the collection of debt. Their only means of enforcement is the legal power of 'seize,' following which they sell the goods of a debtor to pay off a debt. But goods are rarely removed. Normally a threat of seizure is usually enough to make a debtor pay.

The use of private bailiffs is regarded as one of the most effective means of debt collection, where the costs are borne by the debtor. For those on low incomes, the costs are a heavy burden.

A bailiff is someone who is instructed:

- by a landlord to carry out an eviction
- by a creditor to repossess goods under hire purchase or a conditional sale agreement
- to enforce an injunction
- by a creditor to enforce a money debt or a fine

A bailiff has legal authority to carry out these actions. A bailiff can and will try to enter your home and take away possessions which, when sold off, will go towards repaying monies owed and the bailiff's fees. Most people who have been contacted by a bailiff have never been shown a certificate; instead they are shown an ID card. This does not give them authority to take your possessions (levy on goods).

A visit from a bailiff can be a frightening and stressful experience for many, yet parliament is considering granting bailiffs the power to break into homes.

Under the "Tribunals, Courts and Enforcement Bill," bailiffs would be allowed to break into homes in order to repossess possessions to pay for any outstanding debt. Under the Bill, bailiffs would even be allowed to restrain people.

The Citizens' Advice Bureau claim in a BBC article that when they analysed 500 cases "...almost two-thirds of bailiffs were guilty of harassment or intimidation, while 40% misled people about their powers of entry." This alarming figure is without the powers bailiffs would be granted with the Bill.

David Harker, Chief Executive of the CAB said, "Evidence over many years shows that bailiffs have an appalling track record of abusing their existing powers against vulnerable people.

"They are often abusive and aggressive and use threats of violence and prison to pressurise people into paying lump sums they cannot afford.

"This bill would have been a perfect opportunity to modernise the law and end the continual abuse.

"Instead it gives bailiffs greater powers without any proper regulation - a recipe for abuse on an unprecedented scale."

With individual debt is continuing to spiral, how long will it be before we are living in a two-tier system with bailiffs and the state taking personal belongings of millions who cannot afford to keep up repayments on their debts?

The Government openly confirmed that there are less than 1,500 Certificated Bailiffs in England & Wales and also confirmed what most of us already know; that bailiff fees are allegedly open to abuse.

Many bailiffs who are enforcing warrants are charging fees that are not permitted by statutory regulations. Uncertified bailiffs have no real legal authority under Section 78(7) of the Road Traffic Act that says that ("Any person who attempts to seize goods in payment of parking fines who is not a 'Certificated Bailiff' is committing an 'Offence of Trespass' and any person who authorises him/them is committing the same offence." This is a problem that is widespread in the UK.

Chapter 2

Types of Bailiff

2.1   County Court Bailiffs

County Court Bailiffs are employed by the County courts, part of the Lord Chancellor's Department. These types of bailiff are based at the local County Court, enforcing court orders by recovering monies owed under a County Court judgement. They can seize and sell your goods to recover the debt owed and serve court documents.

> The County Court is a Civil Court, which deals with the collection of consumer credit debts and most other debts, which involve a breach of contract (e.g. hire purchase agreements) and enforcement for non-payment of those debts.

2. 2   Certified Bailiffs (Private Bailiffs) are private firms, usually certificated by the local County Court and used by local authorities to collect a number of debts on behalf of the local authority, namely council tax, non domestic rates and rent. They are also used by Magistrates' Courts to collect fines, maintenance, road traffic debts and small tax debts and by the Child Support Agency to collect child support. They can seize and sell your goods to cover the amount of debt owed by you. A certificated bailiff CANNOT enforce the collection of any

monies due under a High Court or County Court orders.

> The Magistrates' Court is a Criminal Court, which deals with the collection of fines and the enforcement for non payment. Civil debts such as council tax, community charge etc. are also collected by the local council through committal proceedings.

2.3 **Tax Collectors:** The Inland Revenue and customs & excise can use their own officers or private bailiffs to collect arrears of income tax and VAT.

2.4 **Non Certificated Bailiffs** are entitled to recover the money owed for a number of debts by seizing and selling your goods, but CANNOT levy distress for rent, road traffic debts, council tax or non-domestic rates, or enforce the collection of any monies due under a High Court or County Court orders.

2.5 **Enforcement Officers** enforce court orders, recovering monies owed under a court order or judgement, or a County Court Judgement passed over to the High Court. They can seize and sell your goods to cover your debt. They can supervise the return of goods as in a hire purchase agreement and the possession of property.

2.6 **Community Police Officers** are the glorified neighbourhood watch. They are the police force's eyes and ears on the ground and have no powers as bailiffs or enforcement officers. They can't even give you a parking ticket; they take names and addresses and pass on the information. That's their job. However, due to the amount of paperwork police have to deal with, Community Officers have been - and are to be given - more powers, yet to be defined.

Most Councils instructs the bailiff to visit between the following times:

- The hours of 08.00 – 18.00 Monday to Saturday
- Or 07.00 – 19.00 Monday to Saturday

Councils vary, so do check with your local council to be sure.

Exceptional circumstances may require visits outside these hours e.g. the debtor may work odd hours, nights, or else no contact has been made between the specified hours.

N.B. Each time a bailiff calls at your address you may incur further costs per visit (added to your debt).

Chapter 3

Asking the Bailiff for ID

County Court Bailiffs: There is no requirement to identify themselves to a debtor. However, if visited by a bailiff, do not let him in your house and ask to see a copy of his Certificate. This should comprise of an ID card, with a Court of issue Seal over the bailiff's photograph and the Certificate, personally signed by a Judge with a yearend expiry date. This should be shown on request. If refused, call the police.

Certificated Bailiffs (Private Bailiffs): If the bailiff is collecting:

- **Fines:** There is no legal requirement to identify themselves to a debtor

- **Council Tax, Community Charge, Non-Domestic Rates:** They must carry a written authorisation from the local authority and show it on request. Decent bailiffs will show any ID or authorisation before being asked

Most City Councils who now use certificated bailiffs instruct the bailiff:

- To introduce themselves to the debtor and show an ID card with photo issued by their company

- That they are to be polite and courteous in all cases

- That if English is not the first language of the debtor, offer interpretation facilities

9

- To show the bailiff's name on documents that are printed and easy to read and understand

- To respond in writing to written enquiries within 14 days

- Visit at least twice in cases of non-contact

- Not to misrepresent the law

- Not to involve under 18s, children of the debtor or non-liable elderly persons in the distress process

N.B. Guidelines differ from council to council.

Chapter 4

Bailiffs' Powers of Entry

One of the myths of the bailiff is that they can come and kick in your door. The bailiff cannot normally force entry into a domestic property. The bailiff can and will walk through an open door, an unlocked door or climb through an open window.

The bailiff <u>can</u> force entry in the following situations:

• Where you have previously signed a walking possession agreement in your home. This will allow the bailiff to return at a later date and take away goods

• Where the bailiff has gained entry, listed and seized your goods, but not taken them away

• If either the above applies where the bailiff has given an appointment time and you are absent or refuse entry

In the cases above, it is the initial peaceful entry and seizure of goods that allows the bailiff to return and use force to enter the property. If you never let the bailiff in, he cannot list your belongings (dependant on type of bailiff).

• The bailiff is seeking entry to premises, which are not attached to a dwelling

"I've voluntarily let bailiffs in my office before now, reminding them that I didn't have to let them in, promising them a quarter of what was owed and came to an

agreement with the rest of the outstanding debt, and I found them to be accommodating." (Normally council tax)

How Goods are Seized

The bailiff will usually try to **"levy on your goods"** or "levy distress." This means that the bailiff will try to gain entry, list and seize your goods. The ownership of the goods is transferred to the bailiff, but your goods are not immediately removed. In other words, "seizure" does not necessarily mean removal. The bailiff now has, what is termed, a **"walking possession."** This means that unless you keep to the agreement made with the bailiff to pay what is owed, the bailiff can then - and will - return at any time at a later date and take the goods away, using reasonable force if necessary, and sell the goods at public auction.

Chapter 5

Which Goods Can be Seized?

The bailiff can only seize goods that belong to 'you,' the owner of the debt. The myth that the bailiff can't seize goods jointly owned is completely untrue. The bailiff can and will seize jointly owned goods, whether or not the joint owner is liable for the debt themselves.

There are some exceptions to what the bailiff can take from your home, namely goods that are hired or rented, because they are not yours. **(Try and find papers pertaining to such items e.g. a hire purchase agreement, rental card, a receipt or a note as proof).** There are regulations the bailiff must follow on other items that can't be taken and are exempt from being taken such as:

- Books, tools, vehicles and anything that is needed and used personally in work or business

- Furniture, bedding, clothes and other things needed for basic domestic, human or animal needs

Bailiffs differ; some will let you think that they can take anything and everything. They can't. If you have a reasonable bailiff, (believe or not some are reasonable), you may be able to negotiate with them, but be aware of what they can and can't take, especially if you have let them in.

The bailiff can and will take things that belong to you and/or goods that are jointly owned by you and your spouse or partner.

The misconception is that bailiffs cannot take goods that are jointly owned by a debtor. The fact is that they can and do. Yet no bailiff can seize goods belonging to anyone other than the person named on the distress warrant. The rules are complex!

Generally, no bailiff can seize tools, books, vehicles or other equipment necessary for personal use in employment or business. However, a bailiff acting for Poll Tax, Council Tax, VAT and Tax may be able to do so.

A bailiff cannot seize goods subject to a hire purchase or rental agreements. However, goods on credit sale can be seized because they belong to the person.

N.B. If the bailiff seizes your belongings to sell at auction, you may/will be charged for:

1. Removal from your property.
2. Going into auction.
3. Use of bailiffs van.
4. Storage (always for cars).
5. Miscellaneous.
6. Any other fees or charges.

All the above will be added to your debt, with you getting only a costings' sheet stating; date of sale, items sold, price each item fetched at auction, bailiff's fees, auctioneer's fees and any other fees or charges.

As you can see, it is better to sell your belongings yourself rather than let the bailiff remove and sell them. You save on all the costs and fees incurred, which you can put to better use to pay off some of your debts.

Chapter 6

Which Goods Cannot be Seized?

The bailiff cannot take the following:

- Goods that are rented
- Goods that belong to another person
- Fixtures and fittings
- Goods on hire purchase

The rules that govern which goods can or cannot be taken are very complex and will depend on the type of debt that is being collected.

- **County Court Judgements, Council Tax and Community Charge**

The legislation states that the bailiff is not allowed to seize the following:

- Clothing, bedding, furniture, household equipment or provisions as are necessary for the basic domestic your needs and the needs of your immediate family

- Tools, books, vehicles and other items of employment as are necessary for your use personally in your employment, business or vocation

- **Non-Domestic Rates**

The bailiff cannot seize the first of the two categories above.

- **Magistrates' Court Fine: They cannot take the following:**

  - Clothes and bedding of you and your family
  - Tools, books, vehicles and equipment needed for your employment

Chapter 7

When and Where Can Goods be Seized?

When

County and High Court judgements can be enforced at any time of the day. However, a County Court judgement cannot be enforced on Sunday, Good Friday, or Christmas Day and a High Court judgement cannot be enforced on a Sunday, unless with the leave of the court. Fines can be collected at any time of the day.

Where

County Court Judgements, community charge, council tax (poll tax), non-domestic rates and Magistrates' Court Fines can be collected by bailiffs anywhere in England and Wales.

Councils generally advise the bailiff that "basic domestic needs" are defined as follows:

* Clothes required by your family
* Bed and bedding
* Cleaning equipment
* Household linen
* A table and a chair for each member of your family
* Children's toys
* Food

- Medical aids and equipment (e.g. walking aids wheelchair etc)

- Items for the care of children (e.g. prams, pushchairs, highchair)

- Heating appliances, except where free standing, unless they provide the only form of heating

- Fridges and freezers, unless empty

- Cookers or microwave ovens unless there is an alternative appliance for cooking

- Washing machine, where there are children, or sick or disabled people in your family

NB. The list does not apply for all councils or other types of bailiff (e.g. County Court).

Chapter 8

How Goods are Seized – The Walking Possession Agreement

The Walking Possession Agreement

The bailiff must initially gain peaceful entry to premises to seize your goods, unless the goods are outside e.g. a car. The goods will not usually be removed immediately. The bailiff will get you to sign a **Walking Possession Agreement**, which gives legal possession of the goods to the bailiff, but which allows the goods to be left on the premises. The bailiff will charge a fee for entering into a Walking Possession Agreement.

The walking possession agreement is:

Valid

- if it is made when the bailiff gains entry and seizes the goods (see 8.2). The bailiff will not remove the goods as long as the debtor makes the agreed payments. If you default, then the bailiff can return, force entry and remove goods

Invalid

- if the bailiff does not gain entry, but instead posts an agreement, with a list of goods, to be signed and returned by you

- if the agreement lists exempt goods, or it is not in the prescribed form

19

If the agreement is invalid, the bailiff cannot return, force entry and remove your goods. The bailiff should be contacted and asked to make a new payment arrangement. If the bailiff refuses to negotiate, the creditor/Magistrates' Court/Revenues should be contacted and asked to withdraw the case from the bailiff.

Clients can request the withdrawal of County Court Bailiffs on written application to the court on court **form N244.**

Case 1

One morning, a bailiff came to my small office to collect **community charge** *(business.) I let the bailiff in* **(peaceful entry)** *after asking him what he was there for and requesting to see the* **written agreement** *(they must show). I explained to him that I did not have to let him in and he said he knew that. (I had no letter from them beforehand and* **no possession agreement was signed**). *On that note, I let him in, listed the two filing cabinets, three desks, three office chairs, two heaters, two computers and other bits and bobs; all my stock, which wasn't much, but amounted to more than the debt owed. The inconvenience of having to buy new stock I wasn't willing to entertain.*

After listing what he thought was worth listing, I **signed** *the agreement. He gave me a copy and the* **fourteen days** *we agreed. We had another wee chat and then he went on his merry way with the* **Walking Possession Agreement***. In situations like these, try and stay calm. If the bailiffs feel confident that you're not going to do a runner and can see genuine hardship and you can come to some agreement, they can be quite reasonable.*

On the other hand, not all bailiffs are as accommodating. Some will, and do, overstep the mark, believing that they are 'God almighty himself' and that you know nothing about bailiff law, (which most don't) and try to run rings around you with fear and intimidation.

Case 2

On another occasion, I had two nasty big burly 'Giant Haystack type' bailiffs call 'round at the office with a 'You can't do anything about it' attitude. After listing my belongings, they found it very amusing informing me that they wouldn't fetch much and would not even cover their **fees.** *Again, staying calm is the key. After giving me the* **Walking Possession Agreement** *to sign, I looked at it carefully and took great joy in telling them that the person on the paper was not me** and that it made the agreement* **invalid.** *Absolutely brilliant, I thought; there is a God after all. The look on their faces was a joy to behold. I shall cherish that moment for the rest of my days, so they had to leave and give the order back to the courts.*

Yes they have a job to do, but you also have rights. **Don't allow them** to erode away your rights with their threats. Know your rights and **always read** before you sign anything.

** They had used my middle name instead of my first name, which I'm known by and it was not the name that was on my bill (the debt they were chasing).

Signing the Agreement?

If the bailiff is **collecting council tax** or **community charge** or **non-domestic rates,** then the person who is liable to pay the debt must sign the Walking Possession Agreement.

If the bailiff is collecting a **fine** or enforcing a **County Court Judgement**, the agreement can also be signed by a responsible person e.g. your partner. **Don't allow this**.

Some Councils instruct bailiffs or collection agencies used to do the following:

- Before a visit is made, send a letter to you. (Some will send two)

- Make a visit, but do not remove goods unless the debtor refuses to pay, or enters into a payment arrangement, or if otherwise instructed by Revenue Staff

- Try and enter into a payment agreement, if you can't pay in full

- Enter into a Walking Possession Agreement making sure you understand, then allow you to read and sign the agreement and give a copy to you

- If the payment arrangement, which is subject to a Walking Possession Agreement is not maintained by you, a warning letter is to be sent before the your goods are seized

N.B. Councils differ in the tolerance of debt owed to them, some fairer than others and councils generally sub-contract the collection of debt to certified collection agencies, so check with your local council. <u>All the above may incur fees with the exception of your first letter.</u>

Chapter 9

Document Sent to / Left with You

9.1. Documents Sent to You

If the bailiff is collecting **council tax, community charge,** or **non-domestic rates**, then you should receive a Notice of Liability Order and/or letter, which states how much is owed, asks you to contact the office to make a payment arrangement and informs you that the bailiff may return and seize your goods and that further costs may be incurred.

If the bailiff is enforcing a **County Court Judgement**, then you should receive a Notice of issue of Warrant of Execution (N326), which informs you of the amount owed, when to pay it by and warns that unless payment is made, the bailiff will call and remove goods. (**People start to worry or panic at this point, especially pensioners**).

If the bailiff is collecting a **fine**, then you will receive a letter or Notice of Attendance, which states the amount owed and informs you that if the debt is not paid then the bailiff will call, make legal entry and remove your goods.

9.2 Document that Must be Left with the Debtor

If the bailiff is collecting **council tax, community charge,** or **non-domestic rates**, then the bailiff must leave a copy of the Walking Possession Agreement, a list of the goods, details of amount owed and the costs and fees charged

Chapter 10

Costs and Fees

It is essential to check whether the bailiff has charged the correct costs and fees. It is not uncommon that incorrect and excessive charges are made.

10.1 Council Tax, Community Charge and Non-Domestic Rates

The fees chargeable by the bailiffs for these debts are the same. The following table is taken from the Council Tax legislation:

1	A bailiff visits your home. Non-entry made. No levy is not made on your belongings	a) £20 for a first visit (£15 for poll tax) b) £15 for second visit (£12.50 for poll tax) c) No further charges for further visits
2	Bailiff makes peaceful entry and makes a list of your goods (making a levy)	a) 20% for the first £100 or part thereof: (e.g. £20) (15% or £15. for poll tax) b) 4% for the next £400 c) 2.5% for the next £1,500
3	You enter into a "Walking Possession" Agreement with the bailiff	Flat fee of £10 (10p a day for poll tax)
4	Bailiff stays with your goods; a "Close Possession"	£12.50 a day (£10 a day for poll tax)

		Agreement	
5	A levy has been made and Bailiff turns up with a van to remove goods	Reasonable costs. A once only charge can be made (Check entry on bailiff papers)
6	The bailiff removes and stores your goods for sale or proposed sale at auction. Auctioneer's fees and other associated costs incurred (vehicles may incur higher storage fees)	Costs incurred not disproportionate to size of the debt Various fees and expenses
7	At auction	Commission of 15% of monies realised and any advertising costs.
8	Debt paid by debtor before sale at auction (no sale)	£20 for inclusion to auction or actual costs incurred up to 5% of any liability order (different auction houses' fees vary)

10.2 What If The Bailiff Cannot Collect the Council Tax?

If the bailiff cannot collect the council tax you owe and there are not enough goods to remove to cover the amount owed, the council will apply to the Magistrates' Court for the issue of a summons for your **committal to prison**.

You will have to **attend court** explaining your financial circumstances and giving reasons why you have not paid. If you do not attend court, a **warrant for your arrest** will be issued by the courts and you could be **arrested on sight** and brought before the court. If you are found guilty, you could face a prison sentence of up to 90 days and still owe the council tax.

Bailiffs are covered by law and have to act legally within the law. If you feel they have not acted within the law, contact the bailiff, and then **contact your local Council**. You should always get independent advice if involving a bailiff. You can also get free confidential advice from your Citizens' Advice Bureau.

If you don't allow the Bailiff in, or if he decides there isn't anything worth taking to pay off your debt, he will notify the Council. The Council may then decide to make an application for your **committal to prison.** This could mean you having to appear before a Magistrates' Court in order for them to look into your financial circumstances at the time of the debt.

The Magistrates will then decide if you have enough money to pay what you owe, or they may decide you are not bothered about repaying your debt. If so, they may send you to prison the same day.

The worst case scenario is that the council may start **bankruptcy proceedings** against you (if you owe **more than £750**). Albeit rare, increasingly more councils seem to be taking this route, so respond to any letters as soon as you receive them. It may give you more time to deal with the problem, but do your utmost not to let it get this far.

Chapter 11

Dealing with the Bailiff

11.1 Contact Your Creditor/s

County Court and private bailiffs act on behalf of creditors e.g. a local authority, a bank and more often now, utilities. Inform your creditor of your financial circumstances and try and have written evidence to back up your financial situation e.g. You have many more debts you are paying towards, no other goods of value, or you are on a low income etc. The creditor may withdraw the bailiff and use an alternative method in collecting the debt, such as a minimum weekly amount. **Above all, stay in contact with your creditors.**

If you know a bailiff is going to call, try your best to have a witness there, making sure you note down what the bailiff says or powers they may claim to have. **Do not let them in.**

Try and make the bailiff an offer. If you cannot make an offer, contact your local Citizens' Advice Bureau who may be able to help negotiate with the bailiff on your behalf. When seeking advice, it's better to have all necessary documents pertaining to the debt and any papers left by the bailiff. Again at this point, **do not let them in.**

Daughter tells of Debts' Tragedy

The family of a woman who allegedly killed herself has blamed pressures created by mistaken demands for £17,000 when she was just £400 in debt.

31

South Derbyshire deputy coroner, Dr Turlough Farnan, said Beryl Brazier's death in April 2006 raised concerns about such debt demands. Ms Brazier, 61, was found drowned in a lake near her home in Derbyshire. Her daughter Susan Musk, from Midway, said better safeguards should be put in place to prevent such tragedies.

'Better Controls'

Mrs Musk, 39, alleged the family had been devastated by the loss of their mother who had been sent demands for £17,000 in arrears when she owed just £400.

She said her mother had been very distressed at the letters and had paid back the £400 she owed the bank, along with a further £100.

"Her death has torn the family apart. She did everything she could to resolve the problem.

"There should be better controls to stop this happening again. My mum can't be the only one who this has happened to. We just don't want this to happen to another family," Mrs Musk said.

Dr Farnan recorded a verdict of suicide at an inquest in Derby.

Woman Suicidal after Losing House due to Council Tax Debt – A personal story

"A Christmas present from the Government; a second harsh lesson learnt after my divorce. In April 2005, I landed a £16,500 a year job. Being a single mother at the time, I thought it was a brilliant job. It meant a lot to me, because it enabled me to get ahead with my mortgage and not struggle to pay my bills.

"I got a job as a Scheme Housing Manager, managing sheltered housing for the elderly, with numerous responsibilities on each sites, including the different levels of staff on site. My new role meant that I could be asked to go anywhere at any time.

"For years I had struggled on in pain due to a bunion on my right foot. It had caused me excruciating pain whilst I was at work and many times I would have to take painkillers just to continue working.

"I loved my job and never took time off. I had a hectic schedule and would be rushed off my feet most of the day. At the end of the day, I could not wait to get home and put my feet up because of the pain.

"Once I had been given a date for my bunion operation, I passed on this information to my employers.

"Following the operation, I was told by my consultant that i would be able to return to work within six weeks. This was not to be the case. After the operation, I remained in constant pain. I could not go anywhere because my foot would continually swell and I could not walk for even short periods.

"When I had my assessment with my consultant a week after my operation, I explained to him the problems that I was having. He said the only other thing that could be causing my foot to swell would be that my foot was allergic to the metal pins holding my toe together. He said that if the pain continued, I should come back and see him.

"The pain continued to be unbearable, so two weeks later I went back to see him. He then told me that the only thing they could do was to do a second operation to remove the pins. I could not believe I had to go through the whole procedure again, which prolonged my recovery.

"Ten weeks after the operation, I was still in pain. I expected to have healed and be back at work. I encountered many problems and when I was told that another operation was required, I was very upset. It was another four and a half months before I was really back on my feet again.

"I was still in a lot of pain and my job involved a lot of moving around from site to site. My doctor said I was not ready to go back, but I was put under an enormous amount of pressure by my boss to return to work. Being under so much pressure, I decided to hand in my notice.

"I managed to live on my savings for about nine months and struggled to pay my mortgage and utility bills. I thought, 'Here we go again.' I knew I had two more operations lined up. I had to sign on and I was demoralised. I had always worked and many years previously, I even went back to work three weeks after the birth of my daughter because my husband at the time wasn't any use or help, but that's another story.

"In desperation, I called my local council and explained to the man at the end of the line that I could no longer pay

£200 a month to help to reduce the council tax owing. He was unsympathetic and said I needed to pay the agreed amount and that was it. I told him they would have to take me to court because there was no way I could afford it, especially as I was not getting that kind of money on benefit.

"The council took me to court. Even when I told them that I could not pay, I was coerced into paying £15 a week, which I paid for about three weeks. When I found it really difficult to keep up with the payments, I went back to the council and was told the agreement couldn't be changed, so I started to pay £10 a week. This was all that I could afford. By the third week the bailiffs started calling.

"I had called the insolvency company on a number of occasions, but they told me that my case had been taken on by a firm of solicitors who would now be dealing with my case. I called the lady in charge a number of times, but she was not available. When she did eventually return my calls, she was very rude and very abrupt. By January 2006, it had taken me about eight weeks of going backwards and forwards from the insolvency company, to the bank, spending money on bus fares and countless phone calls, when I finally got a reply. She informed me that she was going to sell my house whether I wanted it sold or not. This was a shock to my system. Days later, I had people driving past my house taking pictures. The experience was very upsetting and I felt insecure and unsettled.

"I felt as though I was cracking up. I had received some forms from the insolvency company, which I filled out and returned. By this time, I had really had more than enough, so I borrowed some money off my parents took my daughter and went away for a week. By the time we were due back, my benefit of £97 should have been paid into my bank account. We needed money to buy the basic essentials, but I discovered that my bank account had been frozen.

"From then onwards, my days seemed to be taken up by avoiding bailiffs banging on the door, feeling intimidated and suffering from immense stress. It didn't seem right that the government could give the right to the insolvency company to take from me everything that I had worked so hard for.

"I had bailiffs in my house looking to see what was of value to take away, but they then realised that there was nothing of value for them to take.

"By December 2006, I had undergone four operations. That Christmas I couldn't buy a thing for my daughter or anything special for Christmas dinner. It was hard having to explain to a teenager that she would not be getting anything for Christmas because we had no money, but she made no fuss, nor did she ask why.

"I tried to find a solicitor to fight my case against the insolvency company, but to no avail, so I decided it was best to sell my house privately. I had found a buyer, yet the insolvency company tried so many different ways to make me lose my house. The house had already been valued, but the insolvency company wanted the house valued again by an estate agent of their choice. The situation again left me feeling stressed out and suicidal.

"Once the insolvency company were happy with their valuation, exactly what was quoted before, they started to employ further delay tactics, such as changing exchange dates four times and wanting another firm of solicitors to look at the house. They then called my solicitor and accused me of damaging the property, saying that I had ripped out the kitchen out of spite and that the buyer was pulling out because of it. (I knew this was a lie, because I knew the buyer and knew that the house had already been sold). My solicitor could not believe it. After explaining that I had a very basic kitchen of one base and one wall cabinet, she then realised what type of company we were dealing with and the problems I had been having. To avoid the humiliation of being thrown out of my house, I moved out weeks before the due exchange date.

"My brother had promised to help move me several times. I waited and waited in the end I borrowed a friend's car and move what little things I had myself. I was very disappointed. I thought that in my hour of need he would have been more helpful.

"My solicitor whom I employed to deal with the sale of my house had her work cut out and could not believe the nonsense I'd been put through because of the insolvency firm. More nonsense was to come when she got a phone call from the firm saying that they would withhold any access funds that would be due to me.

"Once the buyers had received the keys and they were happy with everything, I requested a detailed breakdown of the costings through my solicitor, to be told that no information would be given and that it would take at least three months before everything would be finalized. By this time, I was close to ending my life and, at the least, having a nervous breakdown. I was now on medication to help me sleep and the whole situation had left me extremely traumatised.

"After my solicitor had explained my condition to the insolvency firm, it took three days for them to send out a breakdown of the costs and insisted on having my forwarding address so that they could send out a cheque of the surplus. I refused to give a forwarding address. I felt that I had more than cooperated with them and, in any case, I didn't really have a forwarding address. My solicitor allowed the insolvency company to send the cheque to her office.

"When the paperwork came through, I cried all day nonstop. The paperwork showed that EVERY single penny had been taken up by the firm. They had used nearly £25,000, which should have gone to me. I could not believe that people could do this and get away with it. It was a devastating and humiliating experience to be going through. The letter had changed everything. My life had turned upside down.

"Everything I had previously owned was gone. All I was left with was a double bed and my daughter's single bed. The wardrobes were built in so I could not take them. I gave anything of use to a friend who was going through a divorce and was left with nothing.

"I had made arrangements to move in with my sister and store items I had in boxes at my mum's. My daughter stayed at my mum's because I wanted her to be settled while taking her exams and she would be more secure. She would be starting college in September. I wanted her to feel safe and settled. I sat my daughter down and explained to her best I could that I wasn't just dumping her, but that mum's house and my sister's flat was not big enough for us both, especially with my brother at my sister's.

"I moved into my sister's and was sleeping on the floor and did not feel contented. I felt that I was in the way. Still with no job, I would leave her flat in the morning about 7.30am and return about midnight (to keep out of her way) to find her cooking. I had a routine and normally I'm in bed by 9.30pm, but because her lifestyle was totally different from my own (I don't drink or smoke), food that I had bought and not opened would be eaten by other persons in the flat. The situation was becoming unbearable and on top of everything else, her obnoxious boyfriend moved in. After a few weeks of not being able to get to bed, I had made up my mind to move out. I started to pack my plastic bags over a few days, moved out to my mum's and slept on her floor. It wasn't until the Sunday morning that my sister realised that everything had gone and that I had completely moved out.

"Life had left me with some severe wounds. I had worked all my life, sometimes holding down three jobs, had been through an abusive marriage and left a single parent with a 20-month-old baby. I paid cash for everything I bought. I've never had a credit card and I don't buy or have anything on hire purchase, so I ask myself where I went wrong.

"I now see things in a different light. I'm stronger and more radical than ever before. I've decided to leave England with new zeal and impetus and am going to try my luck elsewhere. My parents and my daughter are still here, so I will make some visits.

"People who sit and judge me are not the people who matter. Honest family and friends are those who matter. You're fighting a system that wants to break and destroy you and will only accept you once they've taken your last penny and last breath from you. I won't give up and I will never give in, but I will get out of debt!!"

Chapter 12

Bankruptcy and Liquidation

12.1 What is Bankruptcy?

Bankruptcy is a legal proceeding whereby an individual or a business can declare or be declared bankrupt (unable to pay back debts).

If you owe more than £750 in council tax, business rates or an unsecured debt and you have been summonsed, the council may start bankruptcy or liquidation proceedings against you. (Now, by law, <u>any creditor owed £750</u> or more can petition for your bankruptcy).

If they take this action, they will send you a statutory demand, which will give you **21 days to pay** them the full amount.

If you receive a statutory demand, you should **contact your local council immediately**.

If you do not settle the statutory demand, they can and will present a petition for bankruptcy or liquidation in the high court.

If a bankruptcy order is issued against you this will mean:

- all your bank accounts may be frozen
- the official receiver will investigate your affairs
- your home may be sold to pay your debts
- you will lose your credit rating and you will find it very difficult getting credit in the future

If you are declared bankrupt, the official receiver can control your spending for up to three years, although it is more likely to be 12 months.

If a liquidation order is granted against your company:

- you could be forced to sell your home
- your company will be wound up by the official receiver
- your personal bank accounts could be frozen
- you will not be allowed to be a company director for a certain length of time

12.2 Becoming Bankrupt

After a court has been presented with a 'bankruptcy petition', it can declare you bankrupt by issuing a 'bankruptcy order.'.

12.3 Filing a Bankruptcy Petition

You can obtain a form (a debtor's petition) from your local county court (not the Magistrates' Court) for £150, plus a £335 deposit approximately, towards the costs of administering your bankruptcy, payable in all cases. The Court Service website at **www.courtservice.gov.uk** has a list of county courts with bankruptcy jurisdiction. Check out their index of county courts, which will show you the jurisdiction of each court.

12.4 A Creditor Making You Bankrupt

Your creditors can present a creditor's petition. Once bankruptcy proceedings have started, it is in your best interests to co-operate fully, even if you dispute the creditor's petition. If possible, you should try to reach a settlement before the petition is due to be heard. Once heard, it can be difficult and expensive to fight, as there are very few lawyers who will take on a bankruptcy case. Payment becomes the responsibility of the trustee, once a bankruptcy order has been made against you. Your creditors can no longer pursue you for payment.

If you do not co-operate with your trustee in bankruptcy, you could be arrested.

12.5 Where to Make a Bankruptcy Order

Bankruptcy petitions are generally presented in the High Court in London or at a county court nearest to where you live or trade (although not all deal with bankruptcy petitions).

12.6 Who Deals With Your Bankruptcy?

Official Receiver

An Official Receiver is appointed. They act as trustee of your bankruptcy affairs if you have no assets.

12.7 How a Bankruptcy Will Affect You

12.7.1 Assets

Once you're bankrupt, the Official Receiver, or appointed trustee, can sell any assets you have to pay your creditors. However, certain goods aren't treated as assets for this purpose, for example:

12.7.2 Earnings

The Official Receiver can look at your income (taking into account living expenses rent, mortgage and utility bills) to decide if payments should be made to your creditors.

You may be asked to sign an Income Payments' Agreement to pay fixed monthly instalments from your income for three years.

If you don't pay (or if you don't sign the agreement voluntarily), the Official Receiver can apply for an attachment of earnings' order from the court to order you to pay, running for at least three years from the date of an order. In the main, the attachment of earnings' order is what the CSA will use).

You'll need to let the Official Receiver know, if and when your circumstances change. They then can review arrangements made.

12.7.3 Ongoing Commitments

You'll have to still meet ongoing commitments such as utility bills, rent or debts incurred after you have be made bankrupt.

12.8 How Long Does Bankruptcy Last?

Bankruptcy normally lasts for one year (since the Enterprise Act 2002). It used to be three years. After this time, you'll be 'discharged' from your bankruptcy regardless of how much you still owe (excluding fines relating to crimes or court fines).

If you co-operate fully with the Official Receiver, your discharge could happen earlier. Sometimes, in cases of non-compliance, bankruptcy can last a lot longer than one year (where Official Receiver is appointed) incurring higher costs. If you are in receipt of benefits and have no assets to lose, bankruptcy could be your best option.

12.9 Petitioning for Bankruptcy

First and foremost, **get independent advice**. You may consult a qualified **accountant**, a **solicitor**, a reputable **financial advisor** or an authorised **insolvency practitioner.** Then complete the forms, free of charge, from a local court that deals with bankruptcy, or complete forms online. Alternatively, you can print the forms off at The Insolvency Service's website at:
www.insolvency.gov.uk.

The Petition (Insolvency Rules 1986, form 6.27) is your request to the Court for you to be made bankrupt and you must include reasons for your request.

The Statement of Affairs (Insolvency Rules 1986 form 6.28) shows all your assets i.e. anything that belongs to you that can and may be used to pay your debts and all your debts, including names and addresses of creditors with the amount you owe each one. The form contains a declaration of insolvency that you will need to swear on oath before a court officer or a solicitor. In some cases you may have to pay an extra fee for this.

Court staff can only advise you on the court procedure and give you the forms you need. They cannot and will not give you legal advice.

Certain restrictions apply as a bankrupt

As a bankrupt, you are forbidden to do the following:

- You cannot continue the business or a business in a different name

- You cannot form or manage a limited company, or act as a director without the court's permission

- You cannot try to get credit for more than £250 without disclosing that you are a bankrupt

- You cannot hold certain public offices, such as JP, MP, school governor, pension fund trustee, or the trustee of a charity

- You can not apply for goods or services, then fail to pay on delivery

Financially, you cannot do much without telling all those involved that you are a disclosed bankrupt.

Know YOUR Rights

You don't have to let a bailiff into your house. Make sure all the windows and doors are locked. A bailiff cannot come in unless a lawful entry is made (**'gain peaceful entry').** If they cannot get in, they cannot lawfully seize goods. It's that simple. They may, however, try two or three times before passing order back to the council or the court.

You can apply on an **N245** form to **suspend the County Court warrant** to seize your goods and to make an offer of payment that you can afford. The form lists details of your income, expenditure, debts and your offer of payment. The bailiff will not take any further action once you have applied on the N245 form and sent it to the court. There is a fee of £35.00. You can apply on form EX160 for **exemption from the fee** if you are on Income Support, JSA, or pension credit. Others on a low income may get remission if their income is sufficiently low enough. See form EX160 for more details.

On very rare occasions, bailiffs sent from the Inland Revenue can obtain a warrant to force entry into your home.

It's not unlawful to hide or remove things from your house that you don't want taken. However, this **must be done before** the bailiff calls and / or makes a levy on your possessions (lists your belongings).

N.B. If you have any belongings directly outside the house, these can also be seized.

Once the bailiff has gained peaceful entry and listed your belongings (signed **Walking Possession Agreement),** you will be committing an offence if you remove the goods.

Remember:

If you have received notification to say the bailiffs are going to call at your house and take your goods away:

1. You should urgently get advice (Citizens' Advice Bureau is free, but gets extremely busy).

2. Your possessions can't be seized unless you've been sent a written notice by the Authority at least 14 days before any visit. This must have details of any fees added on.

3. You cannot be sent to prison for not co-operating with a bailiff.

4. You do not have to let them into your house. If you don't let them in, contact your council after they leave to discuss any terms or payment agreement.

5. The police have no power to force entry on behalf of the bailiff or local authority, unless there is a breach of the peace.

6. You should lock all windows and doors. Bailiffs have no powers to force entry by breaking in, or breaking off a locked or bolted door.

7. If you let the bailiff in, or they get in by other peaceful means, make them an offer of what you can afford to pay and not what they want you to pay.

8. Bailiffs can only take things that belong to the debtor. If you have a receipt proving that an item belongs to someone else, they cannot take it.

9. Bailiffs cannot have you committed to prison. If they never get in and you do not pay, they will return your case to the court. The magistrate will then look at what you can afford to pay.

10. Again, you should seek advice **as soon as possible.**

Do bailiffs have rights on debts outstanding for more than 5 years?

You may have debts outstanding, but they don't become unenforceable until 6 years after last contact with debtor, so if the bailiffs are trying to collect, they have every right to enforce the six year rule. This only applies to unsettled or alleged unsettled debts without any contact. Once any sort of contact is made between a debtor and a creditor, the six years starts again.

CCJs are out of time after six years without any contact. That's why most credit reference agencies remove them.

Bailiffs are Agents of the Court and have <u>NO</u> rights over your Debt.

If the person you owe money to has obtained a CCJ against you and you have not paid, they can go back to Court (at any time) and apply for the Bailiffs to be sent in.

Bailiffs are officials of the court and would only get involved if there was a county court judgment in place. They have the power to execute a warrant of distress; to seize goods to the value of the debt and costs and then sell them at auction.

CCJs are not statute barred after 6 years, unlike other unsecured debts. They drop off your credit file, but a creditor can still enforce judgement.

If it is debt collectors you are enquiring about, they have no powers other than to remind you of the debt. Any unsecured debt, which has not been admitted to within 6 years, should be statute barred and thereafter unenforceable.

Chapter 13

Help and Advice

If you're thinking about declaring yourself bankrupt, or you're being threatened with bankruptcy, it's important to **seek independent advice urgently**. Some people who face bankruptcy do not take the matter seriously enough, thinking it is just a passing phase with a little upheaval for twelve months, therefore leaving it too late and discovering that professional advisors cannot help because matters have gone too far.

Bankruptcy changes can **affect your whole life for a long time**. The sooner one seeks help, the faster and easier things can be sorted out. In addition, it may be difficult to **find a lawyer** to take your case on.

Citizens' Advice Bureau (CAB)

Your local CAB is a good starting point for free advice. They provide free information and advice on legal, financial and other problems. You can find your local CAB in the phone book or on the CAB website **www.adviceguide.org** for advice, or to find your local bureau.

Consumer Credit Counselling Service (CCCS)

The CCCS is offers free, confidential advice and support to anyone who is worried about debt. Call free on 0800 138 1111. Lines open Monday to Friday from 8am to 8pm. **www.cccs.co.uk**

National Debtline

National Debtline offers free, confidential and independent advice on how to deal with debt problems. Call free on 0808 808 4000. Lines are open Monday to Friday 9am to 9pm and Saturdays from 9.30am to 1pm. There is a 24-hour answerphone service.
www.national debtline.co.uk

The Insolvency Enquiry Line
For general enquiries on insolvency matters, call 0845 602 9848 or email:
insolvency.enquiryline@insolvency.gsi.gov.uk

Her Majesty's Courts Service

Her Majesty's Courts Service is an executive agency of the Ministry of Justice, which aims to deliver justice effectively and efficiently to the public. They are responsible for managing the magistrates' courts, the Crown Court, county courts, the High Court and Court of Appeal in England and Wales.

Clive House
Petty France
London
SW1H 9HD
Tel: 020 7189 2000
www.hmcourts-service.gov.uk

Enforcement Services Association (ESA) (Certified
Bailiffs Association)

The ESA provides a central organisation for certificated
bailiffs and civil law enforcement agents and promotes
ethical and professional conduct amongst its members.

Park House
10 Park Street
Bristol
BS1 5HX
www.ensas.org.uk

National Debtline

National Debtline is a national telephone helpline for
people with debt problems in England, Wales and Scotland.
The service is free, confidential and independent.

Tel: **0808 808 4000**

Financial Services Authority (FSA)

The FSA is an independent, non-governmental regulator of
all providers of financial services in the UK.

Tel: **0845 606 1234**

<u>Help and Advice</u> (Northern Ireland)

<u>The Northern Ireland Association of Citizens' Advice Bureau:</u>

11 Upper Crescent
Belfast BT7 1NT
Tel. No: **(028) 9023 1120**
or
211, Antrim Road
Belfast
BT 15
Tel No: **(028) 9075 2114**

<u>Debtline NI/ Consumer Credit Counselling Service</u>

Debtline NI offers a free, confidential service from budgeting advice to practical debt management plans.

Tel: **0800 138 1111**

<u>East Belfast Independent Advice Centre (EBIAC)</u>

The EBIAC provides a free, independent and confidential advice service to the East Belfast community.

85 Castlereagh Street
Belfast
BT5 4NF
Tel: **028 9096 3003**
Fax: **028 9096 3004**

Chapter 14

Facts and Figures

More Insolvency Ahead

Financial companies predict that people will start building up credit card debt again as hard pressed home owners try to cope with the credit crunch and higher mortgage interest rates. They say a backlog of individual voluntary arrangements (IVAs) could also push up the insolvency figures.

However, the annual report from PWC, entitled Precious Plastic, suggests these trends could change.

"There could be a spike in personal insolvencies next year as a result of over-borrowing by consumers," said the report's authors.

"While the trend in individual voluntary arrangements (IVAs) has declined in recent quarters, this is partly due to a hold-up in the processing of IVAs due to ongoing fee discussions between banks and insolvency providers, as well as fairly flat levels of unsecured debt in the past two years."

Private Firms to Chase CSA Debts

Private debt collectors are to be used to collect money from absent parents who fail to pay child support money. The plan is part of reforms for the Child Support Agency, which Tony Blair says is not properly suited to its job.

In 2006, the agency's enforcement unit cost more to run than it recovered.

Under the plans, the private firms would be able to keep a proportion of the debts they collect, totalling £3bn.

Critics fear that families could lose out as the firms make a profit. They say the CSA cannot even make routine decisions.

Details of the reforms are still being finalised by ministers and senior officials at the Department of Work and Pensions.

Sources have told BBC Radio Five Live's chief political correspondent, John Pienaar, that the decision to sell-on the massive arrears has been taken "in principle."

The private firms would take a share of the collected debt, with the rest handed on in child support payments.

Revenue Role?

Another part of the reforms could see the new Revenue and Customs' agency (the merged Inland Revenue and Customs and Excise) taking on the task of collecting regular child support payments.

This is being described within government as a "preferred option," though not finally settled and is still being debated within Whitehall.

There are worries as Revenue staff are already struggling with problems with the tax credits' system.

Under the government plans, the CSA itself, which one Whitehall insider described as a "basket case," would be given the much streamlined role of assessing cases.

More Bailiff Horror Stories

Single Mum Threatened

A 23-year-old single mum from Bristol was warned that her belongings would be taken away if she failed to pay her £50 council tax arrears, despite having just returned home from a week in hospital with her sick baby daughter.

The single mum who has a 3-year-old and a baby of 11 months, thought bailiffs would offer her some breathing space because she had just come out of hospital with her baby daughter, who had been ill with bronchiolitis. She had simply forgotten to make the latest payment on her council tax arrears.

Not only did they demand the £50 that was due, but an extra £40, which was all she had in her bank account. Allegedly, two bailiffs came round and said they would take her electrical goods, her sofa and a coffee table if she didn't pay.

The single mum said, "I felt really intimidated by them. They should have given me more time to pay. I had arrears of about £1,000, which I was paying off at £50 a month.

[1]Bailiffs Sent in Over 90p Debt

Bailiffs stormed into a Havant restaurant and allegedly told diners to leave because the owner had a debt of 90p. The

57

chef at Lynda Davis's bistro was allegedly ordered to stop cooking and lunchtime customers waiting for tables were sent away. The bailiffs then threatened to seize property and equipment unless Miss Davis paid the 90p she owed the local council, plus £183.10 to cover their costs.

It was alleged that Miss Davis had owed £725.90 to Havant Borough Council in business rates. After the council gave her seven days to pay up before calling in its debt agency, Equita, she paid £725 by cheque, but left off the 90p. The council informed Equita of the outstanding debt and the firm sent 'round two bailiffs to get the cash back.

They allowed Miss Davis to re-open only after a card payment for £184 pounds was authorised over the telephone. Havant Borough Council said it had written to Miss Davis about the debt several times between March 2006 and January this year. Equita says it will refund Miss Davis the £183.10 she paid in bailiff costs, but not the 90p.

[1]Telegraph.co.uk, 13 January 2007:
http://www.telegraph.co.uk/news/uknews/1539353/Council-sends-in-bailiffs-over-90p-debt.html

[2]Bailiff Sent to Collect Arrears of 5p

A bailiff was sent to 80-year-old Alice Nelson's council home in Wigan to demand rent arrears of 5p. The bailiff, who gave Alice a receipt, was sent by Wigan and Leigh Housing, which manages council homes on behalf of the local authority.

A spokesman said, "We apologise for any distress, but we are currently having a strong push to reduce both the amount of rent arrears and the actual number of people in arrears. In terms of how our performance is measured, it's also important to reduce the number of people in arrears, whatever the amount."

[2] The Sun, 13 April 2006:
http://www.thesun.co.uk/sol/homepage/news/article44772.ece

[3]Pensioner Dies of a Heart Attack after Being Driven to a Cash Machine by a Bailiff

A frail 78-year-old pensioner from Accrington, Lancashire, died of a heart attack after being driven to a cash machine by a bailiff who had ordered him to pay an overdue speeding fine.

The debt collector turned up on his doorstep demanding £350, the pensioner had been released from hospital only days earlier after he had had a heart attack and later suffered a stroke which left him in a coma for ten days.

The retired pub landlord said he did not have the money on him, the bailiff then allegedly drives the pensioner to a bank, but before he could withdraw the cash he collapsed and died in the street.

The pensioner, who lived alone in Accrington, Lancashire, had been planning to contest the £60 fine he was given for speeding on a motorway.

In January, a bailiff was sent to enforce an order made by Blackpool magistrates' court demanding the fine plus court costs of £290 or property would be seized of the same value.

[3]bbc.co.uk, 16 January 2009:
http://news.bbc.co.uk/1/hi/england/lancashire/7833530.stm

The Debt Bubble Has Now Burst

Debt is a fact of life for many people these days. Britons have taken on record levels of mortgage and credit card debt, causing concern that people could be heading for a nasty fall.

Facts

- On average, nearly 2500 CCJs are issued every day in the UK

- Over 3.5m people in the UK are long term or permanently overdrawn

- As the debt crisis continues, over 200 properties a day will be repossessed

- The average household debt in the UK is £8,791 excluding mortgages and £53,326 including mortgages

- The average owed by every UK adult is £27,445 (including mortgages). This is growing each month

- The average interest paid by each household on their total debt is approximately £3,400 each year

- Britain's personal debt is increasing by £1 million every 3.85 minutes

How long will it be before bailiffs are knocking down the door of the elderly and taking their possessions? The fact is that there isn't even a criminal records' check for people who want to become bailiffs, so someone with a criminal background could still force their way into your home and take your possessions.

MP's insist they will include legislation to regulate and monitor bailiffs. However, so far this legislation has yet to appear. Under no circumstances should any bailiff be allowed to force entry into an individual's home.

Chairman of the Law Enforcement Reform Group, Philip Evans made claims that the British bailiff is "probably the worst in the world."

Making a Complaint

If you want to make a complaint, find out to which association your bailiff firm belongs before lodging a complaint, then try contacting any of the two listed below:

The Secretary
The Certified Bailiffs Association (CBA)
Ridgefield House
14 John Dalton Street
Manchester M2 6JR
Tel: 0161-8397225

The Secretary
Association of Civil Enforcement Agencies
Chesham House
150 Regent Street
London W1B 5SJ
Tel: 0207 432 0366

.

Chapter 15

Glossary of Terms

Bailiff - Someone who is instructed by the courts to enforce a money debt or a fine.

Bailiff's Certificate - A Certificate that is given to the bailiff once a County Court Judge is satisfied that the bailiff is a "fit and proper" person. The Certificate is a Photographic Identity Card and is personally signed by a Judge and is stamped with a court seal.

Bailiff Private - All bailiffs other than county court bailiffs are private i.e. they work for a company, some on a commission only basis, obtaining their income from the fees they charge for their work.

Bankruptcy Order - A court order making you bankrupt.

Bankruptcy Petition - A request made (by you as a debtor or by one of your creditors) to the court for you to be made bankrupt and giving the reasons why.

Certification - Private bailiffs who enforce distress for council tax (and rent, road traffic penalties, etc.) must have a certificate granted to them by a County Court Judge, who is satisfied that the bailiff is a "fit and proper person" to hold such a certificate.

Creditor - Someone to whom you owe monies.

Creditor Unsecured - A creditor who does not hold security (such as a car a house a boat, etc) for the money you owe.

Debtor - Someone who owes money.

Debts - Monies owing.

Distress Warrant - A writ authorising the seizure and compulsory sale of household effects etc. in settlement of a debt by a certificated bailiff to carry out the process of distress.

Expiry of Warrant - Many people don't realise that a warrant has a "life" of just 12 months from the date of issue. It cannot be enforced beyond that date. Always insist on seeing a copy of the warrant.

Impounding - More commonly known as a **walking possession,** the process of impounding gives the bailiff the power to return to your premises, remove and sell your goods. Goods could be impounded by immediate removal, or by leaving a bailiff in "close possession" of the goods: i.e. on the premises (normally commercial).

Insolvency Practitioner - Authorised person who specialises in insolvency, usually an accountant or solicitor. They are authorised either by the Secretary of State for Trade and Industry or by one of a number of recognised professional bodies.

i-Solv - The Insolvency Service's online interactive website that can be accessed via the service's website, or via links on other relevant websites. A number of insolvency forms can be found and be completed online.

Jurisdiction - The authority of a court to deal with legal proceedings.

Levy - The action of a bailiff seizing goods under a warrant of execution. The levied goods are then considered to be in the custody of the law. It is an offence for a debtor to remove goods after they have been levied.

Local Authority - The council to whom you would pay your Council Tax and Business Rates.

Replevin – To recover possession of goods seized to pay off a debt. Where goods have been subject to a distress warrant, Replevin is a way used by courts to recover those goods.

Seizure - Legal possession of goods by a bailiff who would identify goods to be seized as, or in lieu of, payment of the outstanding debt.

Trustee - The trustee in bankruptcy is either an insolvency practitioner or the official receiver who takes control of your assets. The trustee's main duties are to sell these assets and share the money out among your creditors.

Unsecured Debt - A debt owed to an unsecured creditor.

Walking Possession - Goods have been seized but remain on your premises, available for your use, on the understanding that the bailiff has the right to return to the premises, forcing entry if necessary, to remove and sell your goods if you fail to keep to agreement made with bailiff.

Printed in the United Kingdom by
Lightning Source UK Ltd., Milton Keynes
141455UK00001B/3/P